PERFECT PARENTING

— A COMPLETE HISTORY —

CHRIS CATE

Avamerolton Publishing

ISBN-13: 978-0692872611

Dedicated to the imperfect parents who represent 100% of the parent population. Without them, this book would not be possible.

Craig,
Thanks for being my biggest fan and an awesome imperfect parent!

— Table of Contents —

– The Complete History of –
Perfect Pregnancies

– The Complete History of –
Perfect Baby Deliveries

– The Complete History of –
Perfect Adjustments to Parenthood

– The Complete History of –
Perfect Poise During Unexpected Diaper Blowouts

– The Complete History of –
Perfect Visits to the Pediatrician

– The Complete History of –
Perfect Meals Prepared for Kids
(According to Kids)

– The Complete History of –
Perfect Nights of Sleep Enjoyed by Parents

– The Complete History of –
Perfect Family Photo Sessions

– The Complete History of –
Perfect Communication Between Parents and Kids

– The Complete History of –
Perfectly Clean Homes Where Kids Have Lived

– The Complete History of –
Perfectly Anticipated Kid Illnesses (And Projectile Vomiting)

– The Complete History of –
Perfectly Fit Parents
After Halloween
(Or Before)

– The Complete History of –
Perfectly Calm Explanations of Why Leaving Blocks on the Floor Where They Can Be Stepped on Is Unacceptable

– The Complete History of –
Perfectly Cooperative Kids During Bath Time

– The Complete History of –
Perfect Answers to the Questions Why? Why? Why? Why? and Why?

– The Complete History of –
Perfectly Estimated Distances to Grandma's House That Satisfied Curious and Restless Minds That Needed to Know How Much Farther Again and Again

– The Complete History of –

Perfectly Planned Bedtime Routines That Didn't Go Awry

– The Complete History of –
Perfectly Appreciated Kid Birthday Parties

– The Complete History of –
Perfect Defenses That Prevented Kids from Sneaking Snacks

– The Complete History of –
Perfect Family Vacations

– The Complete History of –
Perfect Days That Began with a Kid Waking Up First in the House

– The Complete History of –
Perfect Distributions of Anything to Siblings

– The Complete History of –

Perfect and Irreplaceable Things That Weren't Broken When Kids Were Repeatedly Warned Not to Touch Them

– The Complete History of –
Perfectly Healthy Foods That Were Entirely Eaten by Kids

– The Complete History of –
Perfectly Effective Incentives to Get a Kid to Make Up Their Bed Every Day

– The Complete History of –
Perfect Weekly Schedules of Doctor and Dentist Appointments and Dance, Piano, Basketball, Soccer, etc. Practices

– The Complete History of –
Perfectly Budgeted Christmas Shopping Done on Behalf of Santa

– The Complete History of –
Perfectly Committed Kids to Brushing Their Teeth Without Being Told

– The Complete History of –
Perfectly Dressed Families on Time for Important Occasions

– The Complete History of –
Perfectly Reliable Kids Who Have Never Lost Something

– The Complete History of –

Perfectly Adaptable Kids Who Had Their Schedule Interrupted

– The Complete History of –
Perfectly Clean Plates and Clothes That Weren't Washed by a Parent or by a Kid Who Wasn't Pressured to Do It

– The Complete History of –
Perfect Games That Kids Played Quietly So a Parent Could Rest Without Breaking Up Fights All the Time

– The Complete History of –
Perfect Amounts of Food Purchased for Kids That Wasn't Eventually Wasted

– The Complete History of –
Perfectly Fitting Kids Clothes That Remained Perfectly Fitting for More Than a Week

– The Complete History of –
Perfect Demonstrations by Parents of How to Always Manage Stress

– The Complete History of –
Perfect Diplomacy During Negotiations About How Much Screen Time is Too Much

– The Complete History of –
Perfectly Crumb-Free Kid Bedrooms, Bathrooms and Toy Boxes

– The Complete History of –
Perfect Family/Work/Fun-Life Balance

– The Complete List of –
Perfect Parents

– Acknowledgements –

1. I acknowledge that there is very little information in this book.
2. I acknowledge that the previous acknowledgement is an understatement.
3. I acknowledge that there are more unicorns in the world than perfect parents.
4. I acknowledge that there are some really awesome parents in the world, including mine.
5. I acknowledge that my wife is a really awesome parent and she makes me a better parent.
6. I acknowledge that it's great when parents strive for perfection, especially when they know it is impossible.
7. I acknowledge that some people will not understand this book, but I hope they will still enjoy it and leave a positive review on Amazon.com as if this is a real history book on perfect parenting.
8. I acknowledge that the word count of these acknowledgements nearly equals the word count of the rest of the book.
9. I acknowledge that these acknowledgements are not what acknowledgement pages were intended to share.
10. I acknowledge that I have read, understand and agree that these acknowledgements need to end.

Signed,

Chris Cate

— About the Author —

Chris Cate has been featured on the Huffington Post's weekly list of funniest parents on Twitter more than 80 times and been recognized for his parenting humor on BuzzFeed, The A.V. Club, Disney's Babble, Scary Mommy, TODAY Parents and many other parenting sites. He is also a regular contributor of parenting humor to the Huffington Post, McSweeney's Internet Tendency, Scary Mommy and several other parenting sites.

Cate is a three-time parent, all-time minivan driver and no-time sleeper. He also hosts the ParentNormal Comedy Podcast, a weekly podcast to help parents laugh when they want to cry featuring interviews with well-known parents. The podcast can be heard on iTunes and at www.parentnormal.com.

Cate's first book *The ParentNormal Crash Course: Everything Traditional Parenting Books Are Afraid to Tell You About Close Encounters of the Baby, Toddler and Third-Year Kind* is available on Amazon.com.

ParentNormal.com